THE ILLUSION OF VALUE

How Brands Make You Pay More

Asa Eccleston Kibilski

Copyright © 2024 Asa Eccleston Kibilski

All rights reserved

The characters and events portrayed in this book are fictitious. Any similarity to real persons, living or dead, is coincidental and not intended by the author.

No part of this book may be reproduced, or stored in a retrieval system, or transmitted in any form or by any means, electronic, mechanical, photocopying, recording, or otherwise, without express written permission of the publisher.

CONTENTS

Title Page
Copyright
The Price Tag Trick: Unveiling the Psychology of Perception — 1
The "More Expensive = Better" Myth: Your Brain on Branding — 3
The Seduction of Status: Why We Crave Logos (and What It Costs Us) — 5
The Science of Desire: How Marketing Hacks Your Hormones — 7
The Placebo Effect of Price: Can a $500 Cream Really Be 10x Better Than a $50 One? — 9
The Luxury Trap: When Exclusivity Becomes Addiction — 12
The Hidden Costs of "Cheap": Why Bargains Aren't Always a Steal — 14
Beyond the Hype: Separating True Innovation from Marketing Fluff — 16
The Illusion of Choice: How Brands Engineer Our Decisions — 19
The "Cult of New": Why We Upgrade Even When We Don't Need To — 21
The Power of Storytelling: How Brands Sell Us Dreams (Not Products) — 24
The Celebrity Endorsement Effect: Paying a Premium for Association — 27
The Psychology of Pricing: Odd Numbers, Anchoring, and — 30

Other Retail Tricks

The "Fear of Missing Out" Factor: Limited Editions and Urgency Tactics — 33

The Social Proof Phenomenon: Why We Follow the Herd (and Pay the Price) — 35

The Generics vs. Name Brands Showdown: Are You Paying for Quality or Perception? — 38

The "You Get What You Pay For" Fallacy: When Expensive Doesn't Equal Superior — 41

The Dark Side of Discounts: How Sales Can Trick You into Spending More — 44

The Rise of Influencer Marketing: Are You Being Sold Authenticity or an Illusion? — 47

The "Fast Fashion" Frenzy: The High Cost of Cheap Trends — 50

The Environmental Price Tag: What Your Purchases Say About Your Values — 53

Breaking Free from the Illusion: Reclaiming Your Consumer Power — 56

Mindful Spending: How to Outsmart Marketing and Make Choices You Won't Regret — 59

Beyond the Price Tag: Finding True Value in a World of Hype — 62

The Revolution Starts with You: A Manifesto for Conscious Consumerism — 65

THE PRICE TAG TRICK: UNVEILING THE PSYCHOLOGY OF PERCEPTION

Have you ever walked into a store, spotted an item you loved, and felt a jolt of excitement when you saw the price? Not because it was low, but because it was high? Maybe it was a designer handbag, a state-of-the-art gadget, or even a bottle of wine with an exorbitant price tag. If so, you've experienced firsthand the curious power of price on our perception of value.

The price tag trick is a phenomenon deeply rooted in our psychology. It's the subtle art of making us believe that something is better, more desirable, or even more effective simply because it costs more. It's the reason we're drawn to luxury brands, why we associate higher prices with quality, and why we sometimes feel a pang of disappointment when we find a bargain.

But here's the secret: price doesn't always equal value. In fact, it often creates an illusion of value. Brands have become masters at manipulating our perceptions, using pricing strategies that play on our emotions, our insecurities, and our desire for status. They know that we're wired to seek out cues that signal quality and prestige, and they've learned to exploit those cues to their advantage.

This chapter will take you on a journey into the fascinating world of pricing psychology. We'll explore the science behind why we're so easily swayed by price tags, the marketing tactics that brands use to manipulate our perceptions, and the hidden costs of falling for the illusion of value.

We'll delve into the concept of "anchoring," a cognitive bias that makes us overly reliant on the first piece of information we encounter (like a high price tag) when making decisions. We'll examine the power of "contextual pricing," a strategy that involves positioning a product alongside more expensive items to make it seem like a better deal. And we'll discuss the role of "prestige pricing," a tactic that uses high prices to signal exclusivity and luxury.

By understanding these psychological mechanisms, you'll gain valuable insights into how brands make you pay more. You'll learn to recognize the warning signs of price manipulation, to question your assumptions about value, and to make more informed decisions about your purchases.

Remember, the price tag is just a number. It doesn't tell the whole story. By looking beyond the price, you can discover hidden gems, find true value, and break free from the illusion that expensive always equals better.

THE "MORE EXPENSIVE = BETTER" MYTH: YOUR BRAIN ON BRANDING

Imagine two bottles of wine sitting side-by-side. One is a sleek, minimalist design with a simple label and a $20 price tag. The other is adorned with ornate calligraphy, boasts a prestigious vineyard name, and costs $80. Which one would you assume tastes better?

If you're like most people, you'd likely choose the more expensive bottle. But why? Is it because you've tasted both and know for a fact that the pricier one is superior? Or is it because you've been conditioned to believe that "more expensive = better"?

This chapter delves into the fascinating ways in which our brains are wired to associate higher prices with superior quality. It explores the science behind this phenomenon, revealing how brands exploit our cognitive biases to create an illusion of value.

One of the key players in this game is the "halo effect." This psychological phenomenon occurs when we make a judgment about one aspect of something (like its price) and then use that judgment to inform our overall impression. In the case of pricing, the halo effect leads us to believe that a product is superior in all aspects simply because it costs more.

Neuroscience research has shed light on the neural mechanisms behind this bias. Studies using functional magnetic resonance imaging (fMRI) have shown that when we see a high price tag, our brains release dopamine, a neurotransmitter associated with pleasure and reward. This dopamine rush reinforces the belief that the expensive item is more desirable, even if we haven't experienced it firsthand.

But the halo effect is just one piece of the puzzle. Brands also employ a range of marketing tactics to further solidify the "more expensive = better" myth. They use luxurious packaging, evocative language, and celebrity endorsements to create an aura of exclusivity and prestige around their products. They sponsor high-profile events, associate themselves with aspirational lifestyles, and carefully curate their brand image to appeal to our desires for status and belonging.

By consistently reinforcing these associations, brands create a powerful feedback loop. The more we see a brand associated with luxury and high prices, the more we believe its products must be superior. And the more we believe its products are superior, the more willing we are to pay a premium for them.

But here's the catch: this belief is often based on perception, not reality. Numerous studies have shown that the correlation between price and quality is often weak or nonexistent. Blind taste tests of wine, for example, have consistently demonstrated that people cannot reliably distinguish between expensive and inexpensive bottles. Similarly, research on consumer electronics has revealed that expensive brands often offer little or no performance advantage over their cheaper counterparts.

By understanding the neuroscience and marketing tactics behind the "more expensive = better" myth, you can start to break free from its grip. You can learn to question your assumptions about price and quality, to evaluate products based on their merits rather than their price tags, and to make more informed decisions about where you spend your money.

THE SEDUCTION OF STATUS: WHY WE CRAVE LOGOS (AND WHAT IT COSTS US)

Picture this: You're walking down a busy street, and your eyes are drawn to a woman carrying a sleek, iconic handbag with a recognizable logo. A surge of envy washes over you as you admire the bag's luxurious leather, the gleaming hardware, and the effortless elegance it seems to exude. You may not even know the exact brand, but you instinctively recognize it as a symbol of status and success.

This scenario highlights the powerful allure of logos, those seemingly simple symbols that have become deeply ingrained in our cultural consciousness. Logos are more than just visual identifiers; they're cultural signifiers, status symbols, and even objects of desire. They tap into our primal instincts for belonging, recognition, and self-esteem, making us crave the products they represent, even if those products come with a hefty price tag.

But why are we so drawn to logos? And what are the costs of this obsession with status?

This chapter delves into the psychology behind our fascination with logos, exploring how brands have leveraged this phenomenon to create a sense of exclusivity and desirability around their products. We'll examine the role of social comparison, the power of aspirational marketing, and the hidden costs of chasing after status symbols.

Social comparison is a fundamental human tendency. We constantly evaluate ourselves in relation to others, seeking validation and measuring our success against those around us. Logos provide a convenient shortcut for this comparison. By displaying a logo, we signal our affiliation with a particular group, our taste level, and even our financial status. This can boost our self-esteem and sense of belonging, making us feel like we're part of an exclusive club.

Brands have become masters at exploiting this desire for social validation. They create aspirational marketing campaigns that depict their products as essential for achieving a certain lifestyle or status. They feature celebrities and influencers who embody the values and aspirations of their target audience. And they use social media to create a sense of community and belonging around their brand.

But the pursuit of status symbols comes at a cost. The price premium we pay for logo-laden products often far exceeds the actual value of the product itself. We may be paying for the brand's marketing budget, the celebrity endorsements, the lavish retail spaces, and the perceived exclusivity. This can lead to financial strain, impulse purchases, and even debt.

Moreover, the constant pursuit of status can be emotionally draining. It can create a never-ending cycle of wanting more, of feeling like we're not good enough unless we have the latest designer bag or the newest tech gadget. It can lead to feelings of inadequacy, envy, and dissatisfaction.

This chapter challenges you to re-evaluate your relationship with logos and the products they represent. It encourages you to question the value you place on status symbols, to consider the hidden costs of chasing after them, and to find alternative ways to boost your self-esteem and sense of belonging.

Remember, true value comes from within, not from a logo. By focusing on your own unique qualities, cultivating your passions, and building meaningful relationships, you can find a sense of fulfillment and belonging that no designer label can provide.

THE SCIENCE OF DESIRE: HOW MARKETING HACKS YOUR HORMONES

Have you ever found yourself inexplicably drawn to a product, even though you didn't really need it or even particularly like it? Maybe it was a pair of shoes you saw on a billboard, a fragrance you smelled in a magazine, or a food item that seemed to call to you from the grocery store shelf. If so, you've experienced firsthand the power of marketing to tap into our deepest desires and trigger our most primal instincts.

This chapter delves into the fascinating world of neuromarketing, a field that combines neuroscience, psychology, and marketing to understand how our brains respond to advertising and branding. We'll explore how marketers use sensory stimuli, emotional triggers, and social cues to create cravings, manipulate our perceptions, and ultimately drive us to purchase.

One of the key insights of neuromarketing is that our decisions are often driven by emotions, not logic. When we see an advertisement that evokes a positive emotion, such as joy, excitement, or desire, our brains release dopamine, a neurotransmitter associated with pleasure and reward. This dopamine rush creates a positive association with the product, making us more likely to want it and ultimately buy it.

Marketers have become adept at using sensory stimuli to trigger these emotional responses. They use vibrant colors, enticing scents, and catchy jingles to capture our attention and create a positive first impression. They use high-quality images and videos to showcase their products in the most appealing light, making them seem irresistible. And they use celebrity endorsements and aspirational imagery to create a sense of desire and longing.

But neuromarketing goes beyond simply appealing to our emotions. It also taps into our social instincts and our desire for belonging. Marketers use social proof, the phenomenon of following the crowd, to make their products seem more desirable. They showcase testimonials from satisfied customers, highlight positive reviews and ratings, and create a sense of community around their brand.

Another powerful tool in the neuromarketer's arsenal is scarcity. By creating a sense of urgency or exclusivity, marketers can drive up demand and make their products seem more valuable. Limited-time offers, exclusive deals, and "while supplies last" messages all play on our fear of missing out, triggering a primal instinct to acquire something before it's gone.

But perhaps the most insidious aspect of neuromarketing is its ability to bypass our conscious awareness. Many of the techniques used by marketers operate below the level of conscious thought, influencing our decisions without us even realizing it. This is why we often find ourselves buying things we didn't intend to, or feeling a strong desire for products we don't really need.

By understanding the science behind desire, you can start to see through the marketing tricks that are designed to manipulate you. You can learn to recognize the emotional triggers that are being used to influence your decisions, to question your impulses, and to make more conscious choices about what you buy.

This chapter empowers you to become a more savvy consumer by arming you with the knowledge you need to resist the siren song of marketing. By understanding how your brain responds to advertising, you can take back control of your desires and make purchases that align with your values and your budget.

Remember, marketing is designed to sell you products, not to enhance your well-being. By becoming aware of the tactics used to manipulate your desires, you can make more informed choices, avoid impulse purchases, and ultimately, save money.

THE PLACEBO EFFECT OF PRICE: CAN A $500 CREAM REALLY BE 10X BETTER THAN A $50 ONE?

Imagine two jars of face cream sitting on your bathroom counter. One is a sleek, minimalist design with a simple label and a $50 price tag. The other is adorned with gold accents, boasts a prestigious brand name, and costs $500. Which one would you expect to yield better results?

If you're like most people, you'd likely assume the more expensive cream is superior. But is this assumption based on concrete evidence or the placebo effect of price?

This chapter delves into the intriguing phenomenon of how price can influence our perception of a product's effectiveness, even when the actual ingredients and formulation are nearly identical. It explores the science behind the placebo effect, a psychological phenomenon in which a person's belief in a treatment's efficacy can lead to real, measurable improvements in their condition.

In the context of consumer products, the placebo effect of price suggests that our belief in a product's high price can lead us to perceive it as more effective, even if there's no scientific basis for this perception. This is particularly prevalent in industries like beauty and skincare, where brands often charge exorbitant prices for products with similar active ingredients to their drugstore counterparts.

Numerous studies have explored the placebo effect of price, with fascinating results. In one study, participants were given the same energy drink but told that one version was a discounted brand and the other was a premium brand. The participants who believed they were consuming the premium drink reported feeling more energized and alert, even though the drinks were identical.

Another study found that participants who were given a placebo painkiller and told it was expensive reported experiencing greater pain relief than those who were given the same placebo but told it was cheap. These findings suggest that our expectations about a product's price can significantly influence our perception of its effectiveness.

But why does this happen? Researchers believe that several factors contribute to the placebo effect of price. One is the power of suggestion. When we see a high price tag, we're primed to expect a superior product. This expectation can lead us to focus on the positive aspects of the product and overlook any potential drawbacks.

Another factor is the halo effect, which we discussed in Chapter 2. This cognitive bias leads us to make positive judgments about a product based on one aspect, such as its price. If we believe a product is expensive, we're more likely to believe it's also effective, luxurious, and high-quality.

Social desirability also plays a role. We want to believe that we're making smart choices and getting our money's worth. By purchasing an expensive product, we can signal to ourselves and others that we value quality and are willing to invest in it.

However, the placebo effect of price has its limits. While our expectations can influence our perception of a product's effectiveness in the short term, they won't necessarily translate into long-term results. If a product doesn't deliver on its promises, the placebo effect will eventually wear off.

This chapter challenges you to question your assumptions about the relationship between price and effectiveness. It encourages you to look beyond the marketing hype and focus on the actual ingredients and research behind a product. By becoming a more informed consumer, you can make choices that are based on evidence, not just perception.

Remember, the most expensive product isn't always the best one. By understanding the placebo effect of price, you can avoid overspending on products that don't deliver and find affordable alternatives that offer the same or even better results.

THE LUXURY TRAP: WHEN EXCLUSIVITY BECOMES ADDICTION

Imagine stepping into a high-end boutique. The air is filled with the subtle scent of expensive perfume, soft music plays in the background, and attentive sales associates greet you with warm smiles. As you browse the racks of designer clothing and accessories, a feeling of exclusivity washes over you. You're not just shopping; you're indulging in a luxurious experience.

This chapter explores the seductive world of luxury brands and how they create an irresistible allure that can easily turn into an addiction. We'll delve into the psychology behind our fascination with luxury, the marketing tactics that brands use to cultivate a sense of exclusivity, and the potential dangers of falling into the luxury trap.

At its core, luxury is about more than just expensive products. It's about a feeling of exclusivity, prestige, and belonging. Luxury brands understand this deep-seated desire and have mastered the art of creating an aspirational image that appeals to our most primal instincts.

One of the key ways luxury brands create exclusivity is through limited availability. They produce limited-edition collections, release products in small batches, and even create waiting lists for their most coveted items. This scarcity drives up demand, making their products seem even more desirable and valuable.

Another tactic is to cultivate a sense of heritage and craftsmanship. Luxury brands often have rich histories and traditions, which they use to create a narrative of authenticity and quality. They emphasize the meticulous craftsmanship that goes into their products, the use of rare and exotic materials, and the attention to detail that sets them apart from mass-market brands.

Luxury brands also create a sense of exclusivity through their pricing strategies. By setting high prices, they signal that their products are not for everyone, only for those who can afford them. This creates a sense of status and prestige that many consumers find irresistible.

The combination of limited availability, heritage, craftsmanship, and high prices creates a powerful cocktail that can easily lead to addiction. The thrill of owning a luxury item, the feeling of belonging to an exclusive club, and the dopamine rush that comes with acquiring something rare and valuable can be intoxicating.

But the luxury trap can be dangerous. The constant pursuit of the next luxury item can lead to financial strain, impulse purchases, and even debt. It can also create a sense of dissatisfaction and emptiness, as the thrill of the purchase quickly fades and is replaced by a craving for more.

Moreover, the luxury industry has a dark side. Many luxury brands have been criticized for their unethical labor practices, environmental impact, and promotion of unsustainable consumption. By supporting these brands, we may be inadvertently contributing to these problems.

This chapter challenges you to re-evaluate your relationship with luxury brands and the products they sell. It encourages you to question the value you place on exclusivity, to consider the hidden costs of the luxury trap, and to find alternative ways to express your individuality and style.

Remember, true luxury is not about accumulating material possessions. It's about living a life that is rich in experiences, relationships, and personal growth. By focusing on what truly matters, you can break free from the luxury trap and find a more fulfilling and sustainable path to happiness.

THE HIDDEN COSTS OF "CHEAP": WHY BARGAINS AREN'T ALWAYS A STEAL

We've all been there, standing in a crowded store, arms laden with discounted items, a triumphant grin spreading across our faces. The thrill of finding a bargain, of getting something for less than its perceived value, is a feeling many of us relish. However, this chapter aims to pull back the curtain on the world of "cheap," revealing the hidden costs that often lurk beneath the surface of seemingly irresistible deals.

While scoring a bargain can bring a momentary rush of euphoria, it's important to consider the broader implications of our consumption habits. "Cheap" often comes with a hidden price tag, one that extends beyond our wallets and into the realms of ethics, sustainability, and even our own well-being.

One of the most significant hidden costs of "cheap" is the exploitation of labor. Many of the products we buy at rock-bottom prices are manufactured in countries with lax labor laws and poor working conditions. Workers may be paid meager wages, subjected to long hours, and denied basic rights. By purchasing these products, we may be inadvertently supporting unethical labor practices and perpetuating a cycle of exploitation.

Another hidden cost is the environmental impact of cheap goods. To keep prices low, manufacturers often cut corners on environmental standards. This can lead to pollution, deforestation, and the depletion of natural resources. Cheap products are also often designed for obsolescence, meaning they're meant to break or become outdated quickly, leading to a throwaway culture that generates massive amounts of waste.

"Cheap" can also have hidden costs for our own well-being. Studies have shown that the dopamine rush we get from scoring a bargain can be addictive, leading to compulsive shopping and a never-ending cycle of wanting more. This can lead to financial strain, clutter, and even feelings of dissatisfaction and emptiness.

Moreover, cheap products often compromise on quality. They may be made with inferior materials, lack durability, and fail to perform as expected. This can lead to frustration, disappointment, and the need for frequent replacements, ultimately costing us more in the long run.

Cheap goods can also have hidden health costs. Some products may contain harmful chemicals or toxins, while others may be made with substandard materials that pose health risks. For example, cheap cosmetics may contain lead or mercury, while cheap toys may be made with plastics that leach harmful chemicals.

This chapter challenges you to re-evaluate your relationship with "cheap" and to consider the true cost of your purchases. It encourages you to think beyond the price tag and consider the ethical, environmental, and personal implications of your consumption habits.

By choosing quality over quantity, supporting ethical brands, and investing in durable products, you can break free from the cycle of cheap consumption and make choices that align with your values and contribute to a more sustainable future. Remember, the cheapest option isn't always the best value. By considering the hidden costs of "cheap," you can make more informed decisions and invest in products that will bring you lasting satisfaction and contribute to a better world.

BEYOND THE HYPE: SEPARATING TRUE INNOVATION FROM MARKETING FLUFF

In today's fast-paced world of technology and consumerism, we're bombarded with a constant stream of new products and services, each claiming to be the next big thing. But how much of this is genuine innovation, and how much is simply clever marketing designed to make us open our wallets?

This chapter takes a critical look at the hype machine that surrounds many new products, revealing the tactics used to create a sense of excitement and urgency, even when the underlying product may be underwhelming or unnecessary. We'll explore the psychology behind our fascination with novelty, the role of influencers and early adopters, and the importance of discerning between true innovation and marketing fluff.

Novelty is a powerful force in human behavior. Our brains are wired to seek out new experiences and information, and we often derive pleasure from the mere act of discovering something new. Marketers are well aware of this tendency and use it to their advantage. They create a sense of excitement and anticipation around new products, positioning them as must-have items that will improve our lives in some way.

This is where influencers and early adopters come in. These individuals are often the first to try new products and share their experiences with their followers. Their enthusiasm and positive reviews can create a ripple effect, generating buzz and driving demand. However, it's important to remember that influencers are often paid to promote products, and their opinions may not be entirely objective.

Another tactic used to generate hype is the use of limited releases and exclusive deals. By creating a sense of scarcity and urgency, marketers can tap into our fear of missing out and drive up demand. This is why we often see long lines and frantic shoppers during product launches, even if the product itself may not be particularly groundbreaking.

But how can we separate true innovation from marketing fluff? It starts with a critical mindset and a willingness to question the claims made by marketers. Here are some key questions to ask yourself when evaluating a new product:

- **Does this product solve a real problem?** Or is it simply a solution in search of a problem? True innovation addresses a genuine need or pain point, making our lives easier, more efficient, or more enjoyable.
- **Is this product significantly better than existing alternatives?** Or is it simply a minor iteration with a few bells and whistles? Genuine innovation offers a significant improvement over what's already available, not just a superficial upgrade.
- **What is the evidence to support the claims made about this product?** Are there independent reviews, studies, or data to back up the marketing hype? Be wary of products that rely solely on testimonials or vague promises.
- **What are the long-term implications of using this product?** Is it sustainable, ethical, and safe? Consider the potential environmental impact, the labor practices involved in its production, and any potential health or safety risks.

By asking these questions and doing your own research, you can make more informed decisions about which products are worth your time and money. You can avoid falling prey to marketing gimmicks and focus on products that truly offer value and innovation.

Remember, the most hyped products aren't always the best ones.

By looking beyond the marketing fluff and focusing on the substance, you can find products that will truly enhance your life and avoid wasting your money on fleeting trends.

THE ILLUSION OF CHOICE: HOW BRANDS ENGINEER OUR DECISIONS

Ever felt overwhelmed by the sheer number of options in a store? Row upon row of cereals, a wall of shampoos, countless variations of the same electronic gadget. It's the paradox of choice – the more options we have, the more paralyzed we become. And guess what? Brands know this all too well.

This chapter dives into the illusion of choice, a clever tactic employed by companies to steer us towards specific products while maintaining the illusion that we are in control. It's a subtle art that involves everything from product placement to packaging design, from limited editions to carefully curated assortments.

One way brands create this illusion is through "choice overload." By flooding the market with a seemingly endless array of options, they make it difficult for us to compare and evaluate each one. This can lead to decision fatigue, where we simply give up and choose the option that seems easiest or most familiar.

Another tactic is "decoy pricing." This involves introducing a third, less desirable option that makes the target product seem more appealing by comparison. For example, a coffee shop might offer a small coffee for $2, a medium for $3.50, and a large for $4. The large coffee seems like a great deal compared to the medium, even though it's only slightly bigger.

"Anchoring" is another powerful tool in the illusion of choice. This cognitive bias makes us rely heavily on the first piece of information we encounter, which becomes a reference point for all subsequent decisions. For example, if the first price we see for a pair of jeans is $100, we'll perceive a $50 pair as a bargain, even if it's still more than we're willing to spend.

Brands also use "framing" to influence our choices. By presenting information in a specific way, they can make a product seem more appealing or less risky. For example, a yogurt might be advertised as "90% fat-free" instead of "10% fat," even though both statements are technically accurate.

Limited editions and exclusive collections also play a role in the illusion of choice. By creating a sense of scarcity and urgency, brands can make us feel like we need to buy a product before it's gone, even if we weren't initially interested.

This manipulation isn't just limited to the physical store. Online retailers use algorithms and personalized recommendations to guide our browsing and purchasing decisions. They track our past purchases, search history, and even our mouse movements to create a tailored shopping experience that subtly nudges us towards certain products.

The illusion of choice is a powerful tool that can have a significant impact on our spending habits. By understanding how brands engineer our decisions, we can become more aware of their tactics and make more conscious choices.

To counteract the illusion of choice, try to limit your options. Before you go shopping, decide what you need and stick to your list. Don't be afraid to walk away from a purchase if you're feeling overwhelmed or pressured. And remember, just because a product is presented as a "must-have" doesn't mean it actually is.

By taking back control of your choices, you can break free from the illusion of choice and make purchases that truly align with your needs and values.

THE "CULT OF NEW": WHY WE UPGRADE EVEN WHEN WE DON'T NEED TO

Remember that feeling of unboxing a brand-new smartphone? The sleek design, the crisp display, the promise of cutting-edge features. It's a rush of excitement, a sense of having the latest and greatest technology in your hands. But did you *really* need that new phone? Was your old one truly obsolete? Or were you simply lured in by the "cult of new"?

This chapter delves into our obsession with upgrading, our insatiable appetite for the latest gadgets, fashion trends, and consumer goods, even when our existing possessions are perfectly functional. We'll explore the psychological factors that drive this behavior, the marketing tactics that fuel it, and the environmental and financial costs of our relentless pursuit of the new.

At the heart of the "cult of new" lies a fundamental human desire for novelty. Our brains are wired to seek out new experiences and information, and we often derive pleasure from the mere act of acquiring something new. This is why unboxing videos are so popular, and why we often feel a thrill of anticipation when we purchase a new product.

But the cult of new is more than just a biological urge. It's also a cultural phenomenon, fueled by a relentless marketing machine that constantly bombards us with messages about the latest trends, the newest features, and the must-have items of the season. We're told that our old possessions are outdated, that we're missing out on something important if we don't upgrade, and that our lives will be better if we only had the latest and greatest.

This constant barrage of advertising can create a sense of dissatisfaction with what we have and a yearning for something new. It can also lead to a phenomenon known as "hedonic adaptation," where the initial pleasure we derive from a new purchase quickly fades, leaving us wanting more. This cycle of desire and dissatisfaction is what drives the upgrade culture, pushing us to constantly seek out the next new thing.

But the cult of new comes at a significant cost. The environmental impact of our constant upgrading is staggering. The production of new electronics, clothing, and other consumer goods requires vast amounts of resources and generates massive amounts of waste. This contributes to pollution, deforestation, and climate change.

The financial cost is also substantial. Upgrading our gadgets, appliances, and wardrobes on a regular basis can put a significant strain on our budgets. We may find ourselves spending money we don't have, accumulating debt, and sacrificing other important financial goals.

Moreover, the constant pursuit of the new can lead to a sense of emptiness and dissatisfaction. We may never feel content with what we have, always chasing after the next shiny object. This can lead to stress, anxiety, and a never-ending cycle of wanting more.

This chapter challenges you to re-evaluate your relationship with newness and to consider the true cost of your upgrades. It encourages you to question the marketing messages that tell you that you need the latest and greatest, to appreciate the value of what you already have, and to find satisfaction in experiences and relationships rather than material possessions.

By embracing a more mindful approach to consumption, you can break free from the cult of new and create a more sustainable, fulfilling, and financially responsible lifestyle. Remember, the newest thing isn't always the best thing. By focusing on quality, durability, and functionality, you can make choices that will bring you lasting satisfaction and reduce your impact on the environment.

THE POWER OF STORYTELLING: HOW BRANDS SELL US DREAMS (NOT PRODUCTS)

Think about your favorite commercials. The ones that stick in your mind, the ones that make you smile, laugh, or even shed a tear. What makes these ads so effective? It's not just the catchy jingles or the celebrity endorsements. It's the stories they tell.

This chapter delves into the fascinating world of brand storytelling, a powerful marketing technique that goes beyond simply highlighting product features and benefits. It explores how brands use narratives, emotions, and archetypes to connect with consumers on a deeper level, creating a sense of identity, aspiration, and belonging that goes far beyond the transaction itself.

Stories are fundamental to the human experience. We use them to make sense of the world, to connect with others, and to understand our own identities. Brands have tapped into this innate human need for narrative by crafting compelling stories that resonate with their target audience.

These stories often follow a classic hero's journey structure. The consumer is the hero, facing a challenge or problem. The brand is the guide, offering a solution in the form of their product or service. The story culminates in a transformation, where the consumer overcomes their challenge and achieves their goals, thanks to the brand's help.

This narrative structure taps into our deepest desires and aspirations. We all want to be the hero of our own story, to overcome obstacles and achieve success. By aligning themselves with this universal desire, brands can create a powerful emotional connection with consumers.

But brand storytelling goes beyond simply creating a relatable narrative. It also involves tapping into our emotions. Brands use a variety of techniques to evoke specific feelings in their audience, such as humor, nostalgia, or inspiration. By doing so, they create a positive association with their brand, making us more likely to remember it and choose it over competitors.

Archetypes also play a crucial role in brand storytelling. These are universal symbols and characters that resonate with people across cultures and time periods. The wise old sage, the rebellious outlaw, the nurturing caregiver – these archetypes represent fundamental human desires and values. By incorporating these archetypes into their stories, brands can tap into our collective unconscious and create a sense of familiarity and resonance.

The power of storytelling lies in its ability to transcend the transactional nature of consumerism. When we buy a product from a brand with a compelling story, we're not just buying a product; we're buying into a dream, a lifestyle, an identity. We're becoming part of something bigger than ourselves.

This is why Apple's "Think Different" campaign was so successful. It wasn't just about selling computers; it was about celebrating creativity, individuality, and innovation. It was a story that resonated with people who saw themselves as rebels, innovators, and changemakers.

But the power of storytelling can also be used to manipulate and mislead. Brands can use stories to create false narratives about their products, to exaggerate their benefits, and to downplay their drawbacks. They can use emotional appeals to exploit our vulnerabilities and insecurities.

As consumers, it's important to be aware of the power of storytelling and to approach brand narratives with a critical eye. By understanding how stories are used to influence our decisions, we can make more informed choices about the brands we support and the products we buy.

Remember, brands are selling us more than just products. They're selling us stories. By understanding the power of these stories, we can become more conscious consumers and make choices that align with our values and aspirations.

THE CELEBRITY ENDORSEMENT EFFECT: PAYING A PREMIUM FOR ASSOCIATION

Picture your favorite celebrity. Now imagine them holding a product, smiling at the camera, and proclaiming how much they love it. Does their endorsement make you more likely to buy the product? If so, you're not alone. The celebrity endorsement effect is a powerful marketing tactic that leverages our admiration for public figures to drive sales and increase brand awareness.

This chapter delves into the fascinating world of celebrity endorsements, exploring the psychology behind why we're so influenced by them, the strategies brands use to select and partner with celebrities, and the hidden costs of paying a premium for association.

At its core, the celebrity endorsement effect is based on our natural tendency to identify with and admire those who have achieved success and recognition. We see celebrities as role models, aspirational figures who embody qualities we admire, such as talent, beauty, wealth, or influence. By associating themselves with a product, celebrities transfer some of their positive attributes onto the product, making it seem more desirable and valuable.

Brands understand this phenomenon and invest heavily in securing celebrity endorsements. They carefully select celebrities who align with their brand image and target audience. They create elaborate marketing campaigns featuring the celebrity using the product, sharing their positive experiences, and encouraging their fans to follow suit.

But why do celebrity endorsements work? Research has shown

that several psychological mechanisms are at play. One is the halo effect, which we've discussed in previous chapters. This cognitive bias leads us to make positive judgments about a product based on one aspect, such as its association with a celebrity. We assume that if a celebrity we admire uses and endorses a product, it must be good.

Another factor is social proof. We tend to look to others for guidance on what to buy, especially when we're uncertain about a product's quality or value. When we see a celebrity endorsing a product, it signals to us that it's a popular and desirable choice, increasing our confidence in our decision to buy it.

Aspirational marketing also plays a role. We often desire to be like the celebrities we admire, to have their lifestyle, their success, and their possessions. By purchasing a product endorsed by a celebrity, we feel like we're getting one step closer to achieving those aspirations.

However, celebrity endorsements come with a hidden cost. The fees paid to celebrities are often substantial, and these costs are ultimately passed on to consumers in the form of higher prices. We may be paying a premium for the mere association with a celebrity, rather than for any tangible improvement in the product's quality or performance.

Moreover, celebrity endorsements can be misleading. Celebrities are not experts on every product they endorse, and their opinions may be influenced by their financial interests. They may also have access to resources and treatments that are not available to the average consumer, making their experiences with a product less relevant to our own.

This chapter encourages you to question the motives behind celebrity endorsements and to consider whether the association with a celebrity is worth the extra cost. It challenges you to look beyond the hype and focus on the actual merits of the product itself, rather than being swayed by the endorsement of a famous face.

Remember, a celebrity endorsement is just one piece of information in the decision-making process. By weighing it against other factors, such as price, quality, and your own needs and preferences, you can make more informed choices about what you buy and avoid paying a premium for mere association.

THE PSYCHOLOGY OF PRICING: ODD NUMBERS, ANCHORING, AND OTHER RETAIL TRICKS

Have you ever wondered why so many prices end in .99? Or why luxury brands rarely offer discounts? Or why that "sale" price might not be as good of a deal as it seems? This chapter dives into the fascinating world of pricing psychology, exploring the subtle tactics that retailers use to influence our perception of value and encourage us to spend more.

Pricing is not just a matter of calculating costs and adding a markup. It's a complex art that involves understanding consumer behavior, exploiting cognitive biases, and creating an illusion of value. By mastering the psychology of pricing, retailers can subtly nudge us towards certain products, increase our perceived value of their offerings, and ultimately, boost their profits.

One of the most common pricing tactics is the use of "charm prices," those prices that end in .99. Research has shown that charm prices can significantly increase sales, even though the difference between a $9.99 item and a $10 item is negligible. This is because charm prices create the illusion of a bargain. Our brains tend to focus on the leftmost digit, so a $9.99 item seems significantly cheaper than a $10 item, even though it's only a penny less.

Another tactic is "anchoring." This involves setting a high initial price for a product, which then becomes a reference point for all subsequent prices. This is why luxury brands often have a few very expensive items in their collections, even if they don't expect to sell many of them. These high-priced items act as anchors, making the rest of the collection seem more affordable by comparison.

Retailers also use "price lining" to create the illusion of different levels of quality. This involves offering a product in a range of prices, with each price point representing a different level of quality or features. For example, a clothing store might offer a basic t-shirt for $10, a mid-range t-shirt for $20, and a premium t-shirt for $30. This creates the impression that the more expensive t-shirts are better quality, even if the differences are minor.

"Bundle pricing" is another common tactic. This involves selling multiple items together for a single price, often at a discount compared to buying the items individually. This can make us feel like we're getting a good deal, even if we wouldn't have bought all the items separately.

"Time-limited offers" and "flash sales" are also used to create a sense of urgency and encourage impulse buying. By limiting the time a deal is available, retailers tap into our fear of missing out, making us more likely to buy something we might not otherwise have considered.

However, it's important to be aware that these pricing tactics are not always in our best interests. While charm prices and bundle deals may seem like bargains, they can lead us to buy things we don't need or can't afford. Anchoring and price lining can distort our perception of value, making us overpay for products that aren't worth the price.

To avoid falling prey to these tactics, it's important to be a savvy consumer. Do your research before you shop, compare prices from different retailers, and be aware of the psychological tricks that are being used to influence your decisions. Remember, the price tag is not always an accurate reflection of a product's true value.

By understanding the psychology of pricing, you can make more informed choices, avoid impulse purchases, and save money. Remember, the goal of pricing is not just to cover costs and make a profit, but also to influence your perception of value and encourage you to buy. By being aware of these tactics, you can take back control of your spending and make choices that truly align with your needs and budget.

THE "FEAR OF MISSING OUT" FACTOR: LIMITED EDITIONS AND URGENCY TACTICS

Have you ever felt a rush of adrenaline when you saw a sign that read "Limited Time Offer" or "Only a Few Left"? Or found yourself frantically adding items to your online shopping cart during a flash sale, worried that you might miss out on a great deal? If so, you've experienced the "fear of missing out" (FOMO) factor, a powerful psychological trigger that marketers use to drive sales and create a sense of urgency.

This chapter delves into the world of FOMO marketing, exploring how brands leverage our innate fear of missing out to influence our purchasing decisions. We'll examine the tactics they use to create a sense of scarcity and urgency, the psychological mechanisms that make us susceptible to FOMO, and the strategies you can employ to resist this manipulative marketing ploy.

At its core, FOMO is rooted in our social instincts and our desire to belong. We don't want to be left out of the loop, to miss out on experiences that others are having, or to feel like we're falling behind. Marketers exploit this fear by creating a sense of exclusivity around their products, making us believe that if we don't act quickly, we'll miss out on something special.

One of the most common FOMO tactics is the use of limited-time offers and flash sales. By setting a deadline for a deal, marketers create a sense of urgency that compels us to act quickly. We feel like we need to buy the product before it's gone, even if we weren't initially interested or don't really need it.

Another tactic is the use of limited-edition products and exclusive collections. By producing a limited number of items, brands create a sense of scarcity that makes their products seem more desirable. We feel like we need to own the item before it becomes unavailable, even if it means paying a premium price.

Social media plays a significant role in amplifying FOMO. When we see our friends and followers sharing their exciting purchases or experiences, it can trigger feelings of envy and a desire to keep up. Marketers exploit this by encouraging social sharing and creating online communities around their brands, where FOMO can spread like wildfire.

But why are we so susceptible to FOMO? Research suggests that several psychological mechanisms are at play. One is loss aversion, a cognitive bias that makes us more sensitive to losses than gains. When we see a limited-time offer, we focus on the potential loss of missing out on the deal, rather than the potential gain of saving money.

Another factor is social comparison, which we've discussed in previous chapters. We constantly compare ourselves to others, and when we see others enjoying something we don't have, it can trigger feelings of inadequacy and a desire to level the playing field.

To resist the allure of FOMO marketing, it's important to be aware of its tactics and to question the urgency that marketers create. Ask yourself:

- Do I really need this product?
- Will I still want it tomorrow, or is this just a fleeting impulse?
- Am I buying it because it's a good value, or because I'm afraid of missing out?

By taking a moment to pause and reflect, you can break the cycle of FOMO and make more mindful purchasing decisions. Remember, not every deal is a steal, and not every limited-edition product is worth the hype. By focusing on your needs and values, you can avoid being manipulated by FOMO marketing and make choices that truly bring you joy and satisfaction.

THE SOCIAL PROOF PHENOMENON: WHY WE FOLLOW THE HERD (AND PAY THE PRICE)

Imagine you're walking down the street and see a long line forming outside a new restaurant. You haven't heard anything about the place, but the sheer number of people waiting piques your interest. "It must be good if everyone's lining up," you think to yourself, and before you know it, you've joined the queue. Congratulations, you've just experienced the social proof phenomenon.

This chapter delves into the fascinating world of social proof, a psychological phenomenon that explains why we're so influenced by the actions and opinions of others. We'll explore the science behind this behavior, the ways brands manipulate social proof to their advantage, and the potential pitfalls of blindly following the herd.

At its core, social proof is a heuristic, a mental shortcut we use to make decisions quickly and efficiently. When we're unsure of what to do, we look to others for guidance, assuming that if everyone else is doing something, it must be the right thing to do. This is why we're more likely to laugh at a joke if others are laughing, to donate to charity if we see others doing so, and to buy a product if we see others using it.

Social proof is a powerful tool in the hands of marketers. They use it to create the illusion of popularity and desirability around their products, even if those products are mediocre or overpriced. They do this through a variety of tactics, including:

- **Testimonials and reviews:** Displaying positive reviews and testimonials from satisfied customers creates the impression that a product is widely used and well-liked. This can be particularly effective when the reviews come from people we identify with or admire.

- **Social media buzz:** Creating a buzz on social media platforms like Instagram, Twitter, and TikTok can make a product seem trendy and popular. Brands often partner with influencers to promote their products, leveraging the influencer's credibility and reach to create a sense of social proof.
- **Limited-time offers and "sold out" signs:** These tactics create a sense of scarcity and urgency, making us believe that a product is in high demand and we need to act quickly to get it. This taps into our fear of missing out and our desire to be part of the in-crowd.
- **Crowded stores and long lines:** A packed store or a long line outside a shop can signal to us that a product or brand is popular and worth checking out. We assume that if everyone else is interested, there must be something special about it.

While social proof can be a helpful tool for making quick decisions, it's important to be aware of its potential pitfalls. Blindly following the herd can lead us to make poor choices, overspend on overpriced products, and miss out on unique experiences.

To resist the allure of social proof, it's important to question the information presented to us and to think critically about the motives behind it. Ask yourself:

- **Are these reviews and testimonials genuine?** Or are they paid endorsements or fake reviews?
- **Is this product truly popular, or is the buzz artificially generated?** Be wary of products that seem to appear out of nowhere and suddenly become the latest craze.
- **Do I really need this product, or am I just buying it because everyone else is?** Consider your own needs and preferences

before making a purchase.

By being aware of the social proof phenomenon and its potential to mislead, you can make more informed decisions about the products you buy and the experiences you have. Remember, just because everyone else is doing something doesn't mean it's the right thing for you. By thinking for yourself and making choices that align with your values and goals, you can avoid the trap of following the herd and find your own path to happiness and fulfillment.

THE GENERICS VS. NAME BRANDS SHOWDOWN: ARE YOU PAYING FOR QUALITY OR PERCEPTION?

Let's set the scene: You're strolling down the aisles of a grocery store, faced with a choice between two cans of diced tomatoes. One is a bright, familiar brand with a hefty price tag, while the other is a plain, generic label with a significantly lower price. The question looms large: are you paying extra for quality, or merely for the perception of it? This chapter aims to unravel this age-old dilemma, exploring the nuances, misconceptions, and realities behind generic versus name-brand products.

The Battle of Perceptions:

Name brands have long held a certain allure. They've invested heavily in building their image, crafting a reputation for quality, reliability, and even a certain lifestyle association. Through clever marketing, they've ingrained themselves into our cultural consciousness, making us believe that their products are inherently superior.

On the other hand, generic brands often suffer from a perception problem. Their plain packaging and lack of advertising can lead us to assume that they're inferior in quality, a compromise we make to save a few bucks. But is this perception accurate?

The Truth Behind the Labels:

In many cases, the answer is a resounding no. Numerous studies have shown that generic and name-brand products often share very similar ingredients, manufacturing processes, and even taste or performance. Blind taste tests have repeatedly revealed that people can't reliably distinguish between generic and name-brand foods, from soda to peanut butter to spaghetti sauce.

Similarly, studies comparing generic and name-brand medications have found that they're equally effective, often containing the same active ingredients in the same dosages. The main difference lies in the inactive ingredients, such as fillers and dyes, which don't affect the drug's efficacy.

So, if the quality is often comparable, why do we pay more for name brands?

The Price of Perception:

The answer lies in the power of branding and marketing. Name brands have invested heavily in building their image and creating a perception of superiority. They use advertising, celebrity endorsements, sponsorships, and other marketing tactics to associate their products with positive emotions, aspirational lifestyles, and a sense of trust and reliability.

This creates a "brand premium," where consumers are willing to pay more for a name-brand product simply because of the brand's reputation and image. This premium can be substantial, sometimes amounting to double or even triple the price of a comparable generic product.

When to Splurge, When to Save:

While generic brands often offer excellent value for money, there are some cases where it might be worth paying extra for a name brand. This might be the case for products where brand reputation is closely tied to quality, such as high-end electronics or luxury goods. It might also be true for products with complex formulations or ingredients, where a trusted brand's expertise and quality control can offer peace of mind.

However, for many everyday products, such as food, household goods, and over-the-counter medications, generic brands can be a smart and cost-effective choice. By looking beyond the label and focusing on the actual ingredients and quality, you can save money without sacrificing performance or enjoyment.

Ultimately, the decision of whether to choose a generic or name brand is a personal one. It depends on your priorities, your budget, and your individual preferences. However, by understanding the factors that influence our perception of value, you can make more informed choices and avoid paying a premium for mere perception.

THE "YOU GET WHAT YOU PAY FOR" FALLACY: WHEN EXPENSIVE DOESN'T EQUAL SUPERIOR

"You get what you pay for." It's a phrase we've heard countless times, a mantra that seems to permeate our consumer culture. It implies a direct correlation between price and quality, suggesting that the more we spend, the better the product we'll receive. But is this always true? This chapter delves into the "you get what you pay for" fallacy, exploring the instances where this adage falls flat and expensive doesn't necessarily equate to superior.

The Power of Perception (Revisited):

As we've seen in previous chapters, our perception of value is often influenced by factors beyond the actual quality or functionality of a product. Branding, marketing, and even the price itself can create an illusion of superiority, leading us to believe that a more expensive item is inherently better.

This phenomenon is particularly prevalent in luxury goods markets, where brands leverage exclusivity, heritage, and craftsmanship to justify their high prices. We're often willing to pay a premium for a designer handbag or a luxury watch, not necessarily because they're objectively better than their cheaper counterparts, but because they signify status, taste, and exclusivity.

Beyond the Brand Premium:

However, in many cases, the "you get what you pay for" adage simply doesn't hold true. Numerous studies have demonstrated that the correlation between price and quality is often weak or nonexistent.

In the world of wine, for example, blind taste tests have repeatedly shown that people cannot reliably distinguish between expensive and inexpensive bottles. This suggests that much of the price difference is attributed to factors like brand reputation, marketing, and packaging, rather than any discernible difference in taste or quality.

Similarly, studies on consumer electronics have revealed that expensive brands often offer little or no performance advantage over their cheaper counterparts. In fact, some budget-friendly brands consistently outperform their pricier competitors in terms of features, durability, and overall value.

The Hidden Costs of Expensive:

In some cases, paying more for a product can actually be detrimental. Expensive products often come with a "luxury tax," where you're essentially paying for the brand name and the associated prestige, rather than any tangible improvement in the product itself.

Moreover, expensive products can create a sense of entitlement and unrealistic expectations. We may expect an expensive item to perform flawlessly and last forever, leading to disappointment and frustration when it inevitably falls short of our expectations.

The Value Proposition:

So, when does the "you get what you pay for" adage hold true? Generally, it's more applicable to products where quality is objectively measurable and directly tied to price. This might include things like high-end kitchen appliances, where superior materials and craftsmanship can lead to improved performance and longevity.

However, even in these cases, it's important to consider the concept of diminishing returns. At a certain point, the incremental increase in quality may not justify the exponential increase in price. For example, a $500 pair of headphones may sound slightly better than a $200 pair, but the difference may not be significant enough to warrant the extra cost.

Ultimately, the key is to be a discerning consumer. Don't automatically assume that a higher price tag equates to superior quality. Do your research, compare features and specifications, read reviews, and consider your own needs and priorities. By focusing on value rather than price, you can make informed decisions that will bring you the most satisfaction and avoid overspending on products that don't deliver.

THE DARK SIDE OF DISCOUNTS: HOW SALES CAN TRICK YOU INTO SPENDING MORE

"Sale!" The word itself is a siren song for shoppers, promising bargains, savings, and the thrill of getting something for less than its perceived value. But beware the dark side of discounts. This chapter will explore how sales, while seemingly beneficial, can be a clever tactic employed by retailers to manipulate our spending habits and ultimately lead us to spend more than we intended.

The Psychology of Scarcity and Urgency:

Sales often create a sense of scarcity and urgency, tapping into our fear of missing out. Limited-time offers, flash sales, and "while supplies last" messages all convey the idea that the opportunity to save is fleeting, pressuring us to act quickly. This urgency can override our rational decision-making, leading to impulse buys we may later regret.

The Decoy Effect:

Another common tactic is the "decoy effect," where retailers introduce a third, less desirable option to make their target product seem more appealing. For example, a store might offer three versions of the same product: a basic model, a slightly upgraded model at a higher price, and a deluxe model at an even higher price. The deluxe model serves as a decoy, making the upgraded model seem like a better deal in comparison, even if it's still more expensive than the basic model.

The Anchoring Bias:

Sales also leverage the "anchoring bias," our tendency to rely heavily on the first piece of information we encounter. When we see an item marked down from its original price, we tend to anchor our perception of value to that original price, even if it was artificially inflated to begin with. This makes the sale price seem like a significant saving, even if it's still higher than what the item is actually worth.

Upselling and Cross-selling:

Once you're in the store or on the website, retailers often use upselling and cross-selling techniques to encourage you to spend more. Upselling involves persuading you to buy a more expensive version of the product you're interested in, while cross-selling involves suggesting additional items that complement your purchase. These tactics can be effective because they create a sense of momentum and make it seem like you're already committed to spending money.

The Sunk Cost Fallacy:

Finally, the "sunk cost fallacy" comes into play when we feel obligated to continue spending money once we've already invested some. If we've spent time and effort hunting for deals, we may feel like we need to buy something to justify our efforts, even if we don't really need or want the item.

Breaking Free from the Discount Trap:

So, how can we avoid falling victim to the dark side of discounts? Here are some strategies:

- **Set a budget:** Before you start shopping, decide how much you're willing to spend and stick to it. This will help you avoid impulse buys and overspending.
- **Do your research:** Compare prices from different retailers to make sure you're actually getting a good deal. Look for price history tools that show you how a product's price has fluctuated over time.
- **Question the urgency:** Don't let limited-time offers or flash sales pressure you into buying something you don't need.

Take your time, consider your options, and don't be afraid to walk away.
- **Focus on value, not price:** Remember, the cheapest option isn't always the best value. Consider the quality, durability, and functionality of a product before making a purchase.
- **Don't be swayed by the decoy effect:** Be aware of the decoy effect and compare the features and prices of all available options before making a decision.

By understanding the psychology behind sales and employing these strategies, you can make more mindful purchasing decisions and avoid falling prey to the dark side of discounts. Remember, a true bargain is one that aligns with your needs, budget, and values, not just one that seems like a good deal in the moment.

THE RISE OF INFLUENCER MARKETING: ARE YOU BEING SOLD AUTHENTICITY OR AN ILLUSION?

In the age of social media, a new breed of tastemakers has emerged: the influencer. With their curated feeds, aspirational lifestyles, and seemingly authentic recommendations, these digital trendsetters have captured the attention of millions, wielding immense power over our purchasing decisions. But is the influencer marketing phenomenon truly a revolution in advertising, or is it just a cleverly disguised illusion of authenticity?

This chapter delves into the world of influencer marketing, exploring its rise to prominence, the psychological mechanisms it leverages, and the ethical concerns it raises. We'll examine how influencers build trust and rapport with their followers, the strategies brands use to partner with them, and the potential for manipulation and deception in this new marketing landscape.

The Power of Connection:

At its core, influencer marketing is about connection. Influencers build relationships with their followers by sharing personal stories, experiences, and opinions. They create a sense of intimacy and authenticity, making their followers feel like they know them personally. This connection is what makes influencer marketing so effective. When an influencer recommends a product, it feels like a recommendation from a friend, not a faceless corporation.

Brands have recognized the power of this connection and are increasingly turning to influencers to reach their target audiences. By partnering with influencers, brands can tap into their established trust and credibility, reaching consumers who are skeptical of traditional advertising. This can be a win-win situation for both parties, with influencers gaining exposure and income, and brands gaining access to a highly engaged audience.

The Psychology of Influence:

But influencer marketing isn't just about connection. It also leverages several psychological mechanisms to influence our behavior. One is social proof, which we discussed in Chapter 15. When we see someone we admire using or endorsing a product, we're more likely to want it ourselves. This is especially true when the influencer is perceived as authentic and relatable.

Another factor is aspirational marketing. We often follow influencers because we admire their lifestyle, their taste, or their success. When they recommend a product, it feels like a step towards achieving those aspirations. We believe that if we buy the same products as our favorite influencers, we'll somehow become more like them.

The Illusion of Authenticity:

However, the line between authenticity and manipulation can be blurry in the world of influencer marketing. While some influencers are genuinely passionate about the products they recommend, others are motivated primarily by financial gain. They may accept payment or free products in exchange for promoting a brand, even if they don't personally use or believe in the product.

This lack of transparency can be misleading for consumers. We may believe we're getting an honest recommendation from a trusted friend, when in reality, we're being targeted by a carefully crafted marketing campaign. This can erode trust and lead to disillusionment with both the influencer and the brand.

The Ethical Imperative:

As consumers, it's important to approach influencer marketing with a critical eye. We need to question the motives behind endorsements, research the products ourselves, and not be swayed by the illusion of authenticity. We should also hold influencers and brands accountable for transparency and honesty in their marketing practices.

By demanding transparency and authenticity from influencers and brands, we can create a more ethical and sustainable influencer marketing ecosystem. We can ensure that our purchasing decisions are based on genuine recommendations and personal values, not on manipulative tactics and deceptive practices.

Remember, the rise of influencer marketing has given us unprecedented access to diverse voices and perspectives. By engaging critically with this new landscape, we can harness its power for good, supporting creators we believe in and making informed choices that align with our values and aspirations.

THE "FAST FASHION" FRENZY: THE HIGH COST OF CHEAP TRENDS

Picture this: You're scrolling through your social media feed, and a stylish influencer is showcasing the latest fashion trends from a popular fast-fashion brand. The clothes are trendy, affordable, and seemingly irresistible. You click on the link, browse the website, and within minutes, you've filled your virtual shopping cart with a whole new wardrobe. But have you ever stopped to consider the true cost of this fast-fashion frenzy?

This chapter delves into the world of fast fashion, a business model characterized by rapid production cycles, low prices, and a constant stream of new trends. We'll explore the environmental and social impact of this industry, the psychological factors that fuel our insatiable appetite for cheap clothing, and the alternatives to fast fashion that can help us make more sustainable and ethical choices.

The Environmental Cost:

Fast fashion is a major contributor to environmental degradation. The production of clothing requires vast amounts of water, energy, and chemicals, and generates significant amounts of waste. The textile industry is one of the world's largest polluters, responsible for about 10% of global greenhouse gas emissions.

Fast fashion exacerbates this problem by encouraging overconsumption and a throwaway culture. Cheap clothes are often poorly made and designed to fall apart quickly, leading us to buy more and more. This creates a vicious cycle of production, consumption, and waste that is devastating for the environment.

The Social Cost:

The social cost of fast fashion is equally alarming. To keep prices low, fast-fashion brands often rely on cheap labor, often sourced from developing countries with lax labor laws and poor working conditions. Workers may be paid poverty wages, subjected to long hours and unsafe working conditions, and denied basic rights.

The Rana Plaza disaster in 2013, where a garment factory in Bangladesh collapsed, killing over 1,100 workers, brought the human cost of fast fashion into sharp focus. This tragedy highlighted the need for greater transparency and accountability in the fashion industry.

The Psychology of Fast Fashion:

So why are we so drawn to fast fashion, despite its devastating consequences? Several psychological factors are at play.

- **The thrill of the new:** As we discussed in Chapter 10, our brains are wired to seek out novelty. Fast fashion provides a constant stream of new trends and styles, feeding our craving for the latest and greatest.
- **The affordability factor:** Fast fashion makes it possible for us to update our wardrobes frequently without breaking the bank. This can be particularly appealing to young people and those on a budget.
- **Social pressure:** We're constantly bombarded with images of stylish people wearing the latest trends. This can create a sense of pressure to keep up and a fear of missing out.

Breaking Free from the Fast Fashion Frenzy:

Breaking free from the fast-fashion frenzy requires a shift in mindset and a commitment to more sustainable and ethical consumption. Here are some tips:

- **Buy less, choose well:** Instead of buying a large quantity of cheap clothes, invest in fewer, higher-quality pieces that you'll love and wear for years to come.
- **Shop secondhand:** Secondhand clothing is a great way to

update your wardrobe without contributing to the demand for new production.
- **Support ethical brands:** Look for brands that prioritize sustainability, fair labor practices, and transparency in their supply chains.
- **Rent or borrow clothes:** If you need an outfit for a special occasion, consider renting or borrowing instead of buying.
- **Learn to mend and repair clothes:** Extending the lifespan of your clothes can significantly reduce your environmental impact.

By making more conscious choices about our clothing consumption, we can break free from the fast fashion frenzy and create a more sustainable and ethical fashion industry.

THE ENVIRONMENTAL PRICE TAG: WHAT YOUR PURCHASES SAY ABOUT YOUR VALUES

Every product we buy has a story – a journey that begins with the extraction of raw materials, winds through factories and shipping containers, and ends in our homes. But this journey often leaves a hidden trail of environmental destruction, a price tag that extends far beyond the monetary cost.

This chapter delves into the environmental impact of our consumer choices, exploring how our purchases contribute to climate change, pollution, deforestation, and resource depletion. We'll examine the concept of "embodied energy," the true cost of production, and the ways in which our consumer culture is driving environmental degradation.

The Hidden Costs of Production:

Every product we buy has an "embodied energy" – the total amount of energy consumed throughout its lifecycle, from the extraction of raw materials to manufacturing, transportation, use, and disposal. This embodied energy often involves the burning of fossil fuels, which releases greenhouse gasses into the atmosphere, contributing to climate change.

For example, the production of a single cotton t-shirt can require up to 2,700 liters of water, enough to meet one person's drinking needs for 2.5 years. The manufacturing process also involves the use of pesticides and fertilizers, which can pollute water sources and harm ecosystems.

The transportation of goods also has a significant environmental impact. Most products are shipped long distances, often by air or sea, which requires large amounts of fuel and contributes to air and water pollution.

The Linear Economy:

Our current economic model is largely linear: we extract resources, make products, use them, and then throw them away. This linear model is unsustainable, as it depletes finite resources and generates massive amounts of waste.

This throwaway culture is particularly evident in the electronics industry, where products are often designed for obsolescence, meaning they're intentionally made to break or become outdated quickly. This encourages us to constantly upgrade our gadgets, generating even more waste.

The Impact of Consumerism:

Our consumer culture, driven by advertising, social pressure, and the pursuit of status, fuels this unsustainable cycle of production and consumption. We're constantly bombarded with messages telling us that we need the latest gadgets, the newest fashion trends, and the most up-to-date home décor. This creates a never-ending cycle of wanting more, buying more, and discarding more.

The consequences of this consumerism are far-reaching. Climate change, pollution, deforestation, and resource depletion are all linked to our insatiable appetite for stuff. The environmental price tag of our purchases is high, and it's ultimately paid by all of us, in the form of a degraded planet and a compromised future.

Towards a Circular Economy:

To mitigate the environmental impact of our consumer choices, we need to shift towards a circular economy, where resources are kept in use for as long as possible. This involves designing products for durability and repairability, recycling and reusing materials, and reducing waste.

As consumers, we can play a crucial role in this transition. By choosing sustainable products, supporting ethical brands, and reducing our overall consumption, we can send a powerful message to businesses and policymakers.

The Power of Our Choices:

Our purchases are more than just transactions; they're a reflection of our values. By choosing to buy products that are produced ethically and sustainably, we're voting for a better future for ourselves and for the planet.

This chapter challenges you to think critically about the environmental impact of your purchases and to make more conscious choices. By considering the true cost of the products we buy, we can reduce our environmental footprint and contribute to a more sustainable future.

Remember, every purchase is a vote. By choosing wisely, we can create a world where our consumption habits support a healthy planet and a thriving society.

BREAKING FREE FROM THE ILLUSION: RECLAIMING YOUR CONSUMER POWER

Have you ever found yourself standing in a store, overwhelmed by choices, or scrolling through online retailers, feeling a nagging sense of dissatisfaction? The constant bombardment of advertising messages, the allure of shiny new products, and the pressure to keep up with the latest trends can leave us feeling trapped in a cycle of consumerism that doesn't always align with our values or our budget.

This chapter marks a turning point in our journey. It's about empowering you to break free from the illusion of value, to reclaim your consumer power, and to make choices that align with your true needs, desires, and values. It's about shifting your mindset from mindless consumption to conscious consumerism, where every purchase is a deliberate act of self-expression and empowerment.

The Illusion of Happiness:

One of the most pervasive illusions perpetuated by consumer culture is the idea that happiness can be bought. We're constantly bombarded with messages suggesting that the latest gadget, the newest fashion trend, or the most luxurious vacation will bring us lasting joy and fulfillment.

However, research has shown that the happiness we derive from material possessions is often fleeting. The initial thrill of a new purchase quickly fades, leaving us wanting more. This is known as hedonic adaptation, a phenomenon where we quickly get used to new things and our happiness levels return to baseline.

The True Source of Happiness:

True happiness and fulfillment come from experiences, relationships, personal growth, and contributing to something larger than ourselves. While material possessions can bring temporary pleasure, they can't provide lasting happiness.

By recognizing this truth, we can start to shift our focus from acquiring more stuff to investing in experiences that enrich our lives, building meaningful relationships with others, and pursuing activities that give us a sense of purpose and fulfillment.

Mindful Consumption:

Mindful consumption is a powerful tool for breaking free from the illusion of value. It involves being aware of our consumption habits, questioning our impulses, and making deliberate choices about what we buy and why.

Here are some tips for practicing mindful consumption:

- **Identify your triggers:** What situations or emotions trigger your desire to shop? Are you more likely to impulse buy when you're feeling stressed, bored, or lonely? By recognizing your triggers, you can develop strategies to cope with them in healthier ways.
- **Set a budget and stick to it:** Determine how much you can realistically afford to spend on discretionary purchases and create a budget. This will help you avoid overspending and make more conscious choices about where your money goes.
- **Research before you buy:** Before making a purchase, take the time to research the product, compare prices, and read reviews. This will help you make informed decisions and avoid buyer's remorse.
- **Focus on quality over quantity:** Invest in fewer, higher-quality items that you'll love and use for years to come, rather than a large quantity of cheap, disposable goods.
- **Buy second hand:** Consider buying secondhand clothing, furniture, and other items. This can save you money, reduce waste, and give new life to pre-loved items.

- **Support ethical and sustainable brands:** Look for brands that prioritize fair labor practices, environmental sustainability, and transparency in their supply chains.

By practicing mindful consumption, you can reclaim your consumer power, make choices that align with your values, and break free from the illusion that happiness can be bought. Remember, your worth is not defined by your possessions. By focusing on what truly matters, you can create a life that is rich in experiences, relationships, and personal growth.

MINDFUL SPENDING: HOW TO OUTSMART MARKETING AND MAKE CHOICES YOU WON'T REGRET

Congratulations! You've journeyed through the labyrinth of marketing tactics, psychological triggers, and the illusion of value. Now, it's time to equip yourself with the tools to navigate the consumer landscape with confidence and make purchases that truly align with your needs, values, and budget. This chapter is your guide to mindful spending, a powerful approach that empowers you to outsmart marketing, resist impulse buys, and cultivate a healthier relationship with your finances.

What is Mindful Spending?

Mindful spending is not about deprivation or restriction. It's about being intentional and deliberate with your purchases, considering the impact of your spending on your finances, your well-being, and the planet. It's about shifting your focus from mindless consumption to conscious consumerism, where every purchase is a thoughtful decision aligned with your values.

The Benefits of Mindful Spending:

- Reduced financial stress: By spending intentionally, you're less likely to overspend or accumulate debt, leading to greater financial security and peace of mind.
- Increased satisfaction with purchases: When you buy things you truly need and love, you're more likely to feel satisfied with your purchases and less likely to experience buyer's remorse.
- Less clutter and waste: Mindful spending encourages you to buy less and choose well, reducing clutter in your home and

minimizing your environmental impact.
- Greater alignment with values: By considering the ethical and environmental implications of your purchases, you can make choices that support your values and contribute to a better world.

Strategies for Mindful Spending:

1. **Track your spending:** The first step to mindful spending is understanding where your money goes. Track your expenses for a month or two to get a clear picture of your spending habits. This will help you identify areas where you can cut back and save money.
2. **Create a budget:** Once you know where your money is going, create a budget that allocates funds for your needs, savings goals, and discretionary spending. This will help you prioritize your spending and avoid impulse buys.
3. **Identify your needs vs. wants:** Before making a purchase, ask yourself if you truly need the item or if it's simply a want. Consider whether the item will add value to your life in the long term or if it's just a fleeting desire.
4. **Wait before you buy:** Instead of making impulsive purchases, give yourself time to think it over. A 24-hour or even 72-hour waiting period can help you determine if the purchase is truly necessary and if it aligns with your budget and values.
5. **Shop with a list:** Whether you're grocery shopping or browsing online, having a list can help you stay focused and avoid impulse buys.
6. **Avoid temptation:** Unsubscribe from marketing emails, unfollow social media accounts that trigger your desire to shop, and avoid browsing online stores when you're feeling vulnerable to impulse buying.
7. **Focus on experiences, not things:** Research shows that experiences bring us more lasting happiness than material possessions. Instead of spending money on

things, invest in experiences like travel, concerts, or classes that will enrich your life and create lasting memories.
8. **Practice gratitude:** Take time to appreciate what you already have. This can help you shift your focus away from wanting more and towards feeling content with what you have.

The Journey to Mindful Spending:

Mindful spending is not a destination but a journey. It takes time, effort, and practice to change your habits and develop a more mindful approach to consumption. But the rewards are worth it. By embracing mindful spending, you can break free from the illusion of value, reclaim your consumer power, and create a more fulfilling and financially secure life.

Remember, every purchase is a choice. Choose wisely, and your spending can become a powerful tool for self-expression, personal growth, and positive impact.

BEYOND THE PRICE TAG: FINDING TRUE VALUE IN A WORLD OF HYPE

Throughout this book, we've explored the many ways in which brands manipulate our perceptions of value, leading us to overspend, accumulate clutter, and chase after fleeting trends. But what if there's a different way? What if we could break free from the cycle of consumerism and discover a more meaningful, fulfilling, and sustainable way to engage with the world around us?

This chapter invites you to embark on a journey beyond the price tag, to explore a new paradigm of value that goes beyond material possessions and focuses on experiences, relationships, personal growth, and social impact. It's about redefining what truly matters to you and making choices that align with your values and aspirations.

The Limitations of Materialism:

Our society often equates success and happiness with material wealth. We're bombarded with messages that tell us we need the latest gadgets, the biggest house, the most expensive car to be happy and fulfilled. But research has consistently shown that materialism does not lead to lasting happiness. In fact, it can often lead to dissatisfaction, anxiety, and a constant feeling of wanting more.

The Pursuit of Happiness:

True happiness, it turns out, is not found in things but in experiences. Studies have shown that experiences, such as travel, concerts, and social gatherings, bring us more lasting joy and satisfaction than material possessions. This is because experiences create memories, foster connections with others, and contribute to our personal growth.

Investing in Experiences:

By shifting our focus from acquiring things to investing in experiences, we can create a life that is richer, more meaningful, and ultimately, more fulfilling. This doesn't mean you have to give up all material possessions. It simply means prioritizing experiences that bring you joy and fulfillment over accumulating things you don't need.

The Power of Connection:

Relationships are another key source of happiness and well-being. Studies have shown that strong social connections are essential for our mental and physical health. By investing in our relationships with family, friends, and loved ones, we can create a support network that provides us with love, comfort, and belonging.

Personal Growth and Purpose:

Another important aspect of finding true value is personal growth and the pursuit of purpose. When we engage in activities that challenge us, teach us new things, and contribute to our personal development, we experience a sense of accomplishment and fulfillment that goes far beyond material possessions.

Finding your purpose may involve volunteering for a cause you care about, pursuing a creative passion, or simply learning a new skill. Whatever it is, engaging in activities that give you a sense of meaning and contribution can bring a deep sense of satisfaction and well-being.

Social Impact:

Finally, consider the impact of your purchases on the world around you. By choosing to buy from ethical and sustainable brands, you're not just getting a product; you're supporting companies that prioritize fair labor practices, environmental sustainability, and social responsibility. You're also sending a message to other businesses that consumers care about these issues.

By making conscious consumer choices, you can use your purchasing power to create positive change in the world. This can bring a sense of purpose and fulfillment that extends far beyond the individual transaction.

The Journey to True Value:

Finding true value in a world of hype is a journey, not a destination. It requires a shift in mindset, a willingness to question our assumptions, and a commitment to making choices that align with our values and aspirations. But the rewards are immeasurable.

By embracing this new paradigm of value, you can break free from the illusion of materialism, create a life that is richer, more meaningful, and more sustainable. You can discover that true happiness is not found in things, but in experiences, relationships, personal growth, and social impact.

THE REVOLUTION STARTS WITH YOU: A MANIFESTO FOR CONSCIOUS CONSUMERISM

You've reached the final chapter of our journey, armed with a new understanding of the illusion of value, the tactics used to manipulate our desires, and the power we hold as consumers. This chapter is your call to action, a manifesto for conscious consumerism that empowers you to create a more sustainable, ethical, and fulfilling future for yourself and the planet.

The Power of One:

It's easy to feel overwhelmed by the challenges facing our world, to believe that our individual actions are insignificant in the face of global problems. But the truth is, every choice we make as consumers has an impact. Every dollar we spend is a vote for the kind of world we want to live in.

By choosing to buy from ethical and sustainable brands, we support businesses that prioritize fair labor practices, environmental sustainability, and social responsibility. By refusing to buy products that are produced unethically or contribute to environmental degradation, we send a message to corporations that we demand better.

Your voice matters. Your choices matter. The revolution starts with you.

A Manifesto for Conscious Consumerism:

1. **Educate Yourself:** Learn about the social and environmental impact of your purchases. Research brands, read labels, and ask questions. The more you know, the more informed decisions you can make.

2. **Prioritize Quality Over Quantity:** Invest in fewer, higher-quality items that will last longer and bring you more joy than a closet full of cheap, disposable goods.
3. **Support Ethical and Sustainable Brands:** Seek out brands that are transparent about their supply chains, prioritize fair labor practices, and use sustainable materials.
4. **Buy Secondhand:** Give pre-loved items a new life by shopping at thrift stores, consignment shops, and online marketplaces.
5. **Repair, Don't Replace:** Learn to mend and repair your belongings instead of throwing them away and buying new ones.
6. **Reduce, Reuse, Recycle:** Minimize waste by reducing your consumption, reusing items whenever possible, and recycling what you can't reuse.
7. **Vote with Your Wallet:** Every purchase is a vote for the kind of world you want to live in. Choose to support businesses that align with your values.
8. **Speak Up:** Share your concerns with brands and retailers. Let them know that you care about ethical and sustainable practices.
9. **Spread the Word:** Talk to your friends and family about conscious consumerism. The more people who embrace this mindset, the greater the impact we can have.
10. **Be Patient and Kind to Yourself:** Changing your habits takes time and effort. Don't be discouraged if you slip up occasionally. The most important thing is to keep learning and growing.

The Future We Create:

By embracing conscious consumerism, we can create a world where our purchases reflect our values, where businesses are held accountable for their impact on people and the planet, and where our consumption habits contribute to a more just, equitable, and sustainable future.

The revolution starts with you. The choices you make today will shape the world of tomorrow. Choose wisely, and together, we can build a brighter future for all.

www.ingramcontent.com/pod-product-compliance
Lightning Source LLC
Chambersburg PA
CBHW071956210526
45479CB00003B/955